D0202286

American Lives

Elizabeth
Cady Stanton

Heidi Moore

Heinemann Library
Chicago, Illinois

Designed by Heinemann Library
Photo research by Eva Schorr
Printed in China by WKT Company Limited.

08 07 06 05 04
10 9 8 7 6 5 4 3 2 1

Library of Congress Cataloging-in-Publication Data
Moore, Heidi, 1976-
  Elizabeth Cady Stanton / Heidi Moore.
    v. cm. -- (American lives (Heinemann Library (Firm)))
Includes bibliographical references and index.
Contents: Rights for Women -- Childhood -- Education -- Growing Up -- First years of marriage -- Seneca Falls -- Meeting Susan B. Anthony -- Children and work -- Suffrage -- The Civil War -- More work to do -- Her last years -- Remembering Stanton. ISBN 1-4034-4994-5 (Hardcover) -- ISBN 1-4034-5705-0 (Paperback)
  1. Stanton, Elizabeth Cady, 1815-1902--Juvenile literature. 2. Feminists--United States--Biography--Juvenile literature. 3. Women's rights--United States--History--19th century--Juvenile literature. [1. Stanton, Elizabeth Cady, 1815-1902. 2. Suffragists. 3. Women's rights. 4. Women--Biography.] I. Title. II. Series.
  HQ1413.S67M66 2003
  305.42'092--dc22

2003015751

Acknowledgments
The author and publishers are grateful to the following for permission to reproduce copyright material: Title page, pp. 5, 16, 23, 24 Bettmann/Corbis; p. 4 Sophia Smith Collection/Smith College Library; pp. 6, 11 Vassar College Library; pp. 7, 8, 17, 19 Coline Jenkins-Sahlin; p. 9 Courtesy of the National Register of Historic Places, photo by John Harwood pp. 10, 15, 21, 29 Library of Congress; p. 12 National Portrait Gallery/Smithsonian Institution/Art Resource, NY; p. 13 North Wind Picture Archives; pp. 14, 15 Women's Rights National Historical Park; pp. 18, 20, 25, 26, 27, 28 Corbis

Cover photograph by Bettmann/Corbis

The author would like to thank her husband James and her editor, Angela McHaney Brown.

The publisher would like to thank Michelle Rimsa for her comments in the preparation of this book.

Every effort has been made to contact copyright holders of any material reproduced in this book. Any omissions will be rectified in subsequent printings if notice is given to the publisher.

The cover image of Elizabeth Cady Stanton was taken in the 1880s. She was about 70 years old.

Contents

Some words are shown in bold, **like this.** You can find out what they mean by looking in the glossary.

Rights for Women

Elizabeth Cady grew up in the early 1800s. At that time, women in the United States could not vote. Elizabeth thought this was unfair. She believed girls were as smart and as strong as boys. She also thought women should have the same rights as men. But at the time, there were many laws that were unfair to women.

Elizabeth decided to try to change the laws. This fight for **equality** would take the rest of her life.

Elizabeth became one of the most famous women of her time. She is shown here at age twenty.

Elizabeth Cady would become one of the first members of the women's movement. She would work with other women, and men, to change unfair laws.

During her entire life, Elizabeth fought for women to own property and vote. She became a strong leader and inspired other women to join her fight for equality.

Elizabeth gave many lectures about women's rights. She also discussed how to raise a family and why slavery needed to be ended.

Childhood

Elizabeth Cady was born on November 12, 1815, in Johnstown, New York. She came from a powerful family. Her father, Daniel Cady, was a member of the U.S. Congress and later a New York Supreme Court judge. Her mother's father had fought in the Revolutionary War, the war for independence from Great Britain.

Elizabeth's mother, Margaret Livingston Cady, came from an important family.

The Life of Elizabeth Cady Stanton

1815	1830	1848	1851
Born on November 12 in Johnstown, New York	Started at Emma Willard's Seminary	Held Seneca Falls Convention on July 19 and 20	Met Susan B. Anthony

This is where Elizabeth lived with her parents in Johnstown, New York.

Elizabeth's family had a lot of money. She lived in a big house, and there were servants to do the housework. Elizabeth was one of ten children, but only five of them lived to be adults. Many children at the time died of disease because of poor medical care.

As a child, Elizabeth loved reading and was very curious. She loved playing dress-up with the family's old costumes.

1860	1869	1878	1902
Helped pass Married Women's Property Act	*Founded National Woman Suffrage Association*	*Spoke in front of Congress*	*Died on October 26*

Education

When Elizabeth was eleven years old, her older brother Eleazar died. This upset Elizabeth very much, and she knew her father was very sad, too.

She wanted to make her father feel better, so Elizabeth told him that she would try to be everything her brother had been. She made a promise to be as smart, strong, and brave as Eleazar was.

Daniel Cady was respected as a lawyer, judge, and New York congressman.

Childhood memory

When Elizabeth's brother died, her father said, "Oh, my daughter, I wish you were a boy!" She replied, "I will try to be all my brother was."

Elizabeth started riding horses and learned to leap over fences on horseback. When she was eleven, she went to Johnstown Academy, a **co-ed** school for boys and girls. Elizabeth was the only girl in her class. She studied Latin, Greek, and mathematics. She worked hard and became one of the best students. One year she won the second prize in Greek.

Emma Willard's Seminary in Troy, New York, was a school for girls only.

When it was time to go to college, most of the boys from Johnstown Academy went to Union College in Schenectady, New York. Union College was not co-ed, so Elizabeth could not go there. She instead went to Emma Willard's **Seminary.**

Growing Up

At first Elizabeth was not happy to be at the **seminary** in Troy. She missed her old friends from Johnstown Academy. But soon she was excited about learning new things and seeing new places. She studied French, music, and dancing.

Elizabeth's cousin Gerrit Smith worked to end slavery.

When Elizabeth was 23, she started spending time at her cousin Gerrit Smith's house in Peterboro, New York. Smith was an **abolitionist,** which means that he wanted to end slavery. During slavery, people were allowed to buy and sell other human beings and force them to work without pay. Elizabeth heard about the hard lives of the slaves and soon joined the fight to end slavery.

This is a photo of Henry Brewster Stanton taken many years after he married Elizabeth.

At the Smiths' house in 1839, Elizabeth met a young man named Henry Brewster Stanton, an abolitionist. Soon he and Elizabeth fell in love. He asked her to marry him, and she said yes.

But her father did not want them to marry, so she changed her mind. Stanton sent her letters for months until, finally, in the spring of 1840, she married him.

First Years of Marriage

Elizabeth Cady was 24 years old when she married Henry. She changed her name to Elizabeth Cady Stanton.

Right after they were married, Elizabeth and her new husband went to the World's Anti-Slavery **Convention,** a big meeting held in London, England. The fact that women were not allowed to speak during the meeting made Elizabeth furious. Two years after she returned to the United States, she started working for women's rights and **equality.**

At the convention in London, Elizabeth met Lucretia Mott. She was an important **feminist** and a leader in the American women's movement.

This is how Boston looked around
the time Elizabeth moved there.

During the first few years of marriage,
the Stantons lived with Elizabeth's parents.
Then they moved to Boston, Massachusetts.
Elizabeth liked the excitement of city life.

The Stantons had servants, so Elizabeth
did not have to do much **domestic** work
like cleaning or sewing. From 1842 to 1845
she gave birth to three boys, named Daniel,
Henry, and Gerrit.

Seneca Falls

In 1847 Henry's poor health led the family to move to Seneca Falls, New York. They lived there until 1862. They had only two new, poorly trained servants, so Elizabeth spent a lot more time doing **domestic** work. At first, she missed her Boston friends and was unhappy.

This is where Elizabeth raised her children and began the women's rights movement.

But soon after the move, Elizabeth found out Lucretia Mott was staying near Seneca Falls. The two women began to hold meetings about the women's movement.

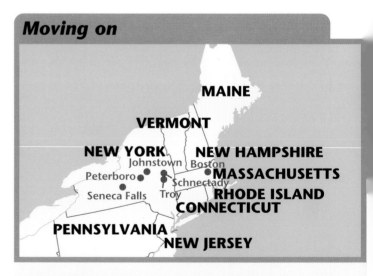

Elizabeth lived in small towns in New York state.

The Seneca Falls **Convention** took place on July 19 and 20, 1848. It was the first large meeting held in the United States focused on women's rights. At the convention, Mott and Stanton had men and women sign a **pledge** based on the Declaration of Independence.

This is the house where the Declaration of Sentiments was written.

It said that women should have the right to own their own property, to keep the pay they earned from their jobs, and to have **custody,** or the legal right to take care of, their children. The most shocking thing they asked for was the right to vote. The pledge led to the state of New York passing the Married Women's Property Act in 1848. The Act gave women the right to own property.

Meeting Susan B. Anthony

After the Seneca Falls Convention, Elizabeth became known as a leader in the women's movement. Another leader working for women's rights was Susan B. Anthony.

Elizabeth and Susan met in 1851, and their friendship became an important part of their lives. Both were strong, courageous women. Together they were even stronger. They would work together for more than 50 years.

Elizabeth and Susan worked well together. Susan was a talented thinker and writer, and Elizabeth was a very good speaker.

Susan learned about the law from Elizabeth, who had read her father's law books when she was younger. Together they wrote letters to change laws in the state of New York to allow married women to own property.

Elizabeth's son Theodore was born in 1851, and her daughter Margaret was born in 1852.

At the time, women's property was given to their husbands when they got married. Women also had no legal right to their children. Only fathers could have **custody.**

Elizabeth and Susan both thought this was wrong. In 1854, Elizabeth spoke in front of the New York state **legislature.** She explained why they should change the laws.

Children and Work

By 1859 Elizabeth had seven children. Her last two were a daughter, Harriot, and a son, Robert. Although she loved her family, Elizabeth found it hard to work for women's rights while raising children.

"BLOOMERISM,"
OR THE
NEW FEMALE COSTUME OF 1851,

As it has appeared in the various Cities and Towns.

BOSTON: S. W. WHEELER, 66 Cornhill—1851.

Her husband Henry's work kept him away from home a lot. So most of the **domestic** duties like cooking, cleaning, and taking care of the children fell to Elizabeth.

Elizabeth started wearing **bloomers** instead of long skirts in the 1850s. The short skirt over long pants made it easier to move around and do housework.

Elizabeth once said she felt like a "caged lion," trapped within the four walls of her home. Luckily, she had Susan B. Anthony to help her spread her ideas. Elizabeth wrote letters and speeches, and then Susan traveled around the country sharing their beliefs about **equality.**

Elizabeth is shown here with two of her sons, Henry and Daniel.

Ideas about children

*Elizabeth had **radical** ideas about taking care of her children. She gave them baths every day and encouraged them to play outside in the fresh air and sunshine. In the 1850s, people thought those were bad ideas!*

Suffrage

Stanton and Anthony's hard work paid off. The Married Women's Property Act of 1848 was extended in 1860. It gave married women the right to own property, to keep the pay they earned from their jobs, and to have **custody** of their children. But women still did not have the right to vote.

Stanton is shown here with her daughter Harriot.

Some people did not like the idea of women's suffrage. This 1850s cartoon is making fun of the **suffragists,** including Stanton.

Stanton still believed strongly in the importance of women's **suffrage.** She also wanted **emancipation,** or freedom, for the slaves. Many **abolitionists** such as Frederick Douglass, William Lloyd Garrison, and Stanton's cousin Gerrit Smith also worked to get rights for women. But not all abolitionists thought women should be able to vote.

The Civil War

In 1861, the Civil War started. The southern states broke away from the northern states because the South did not want to give up slavery.

Stanton and Anthony worked to end slavery. In 1863, they started the National Woman's Loyal League, which collected 300,000 signatures to help pass a law to **emancipate** slaves. Later that year, President Abraham Lincoln signed the Emancipation Proclamation, which called for an end to slavery in the South.

During the Civil War

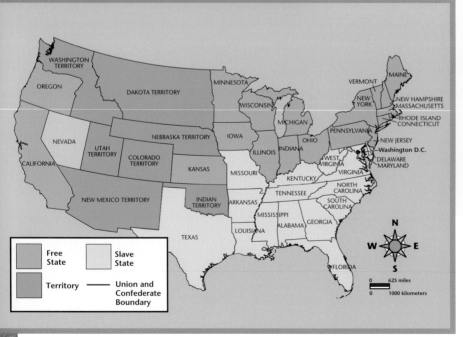

Free State
Slave State
Territory
Union and Confederate Boundary

From 1861 to 1865, the country was split into the North and South.

Frederick Douglass was one of the leaders of the abolitionist movement.

While the country was at war over slavery, Stanton and Anthony were at war with their old friends over the vote for women. Some of the **abolitionists** asked for the vote for freed male slaves, but left out women. Stanton and Anthony wanted everyone, including women, to be able to vote.

Stanton and Anthony were angry and hurt. They felt left behind. In 1869 they started the National Woman **Suffrage** Association to continue the fight for women's right to vote. Stanton was the association's president.

More Work To Do

After women were passed over for the right to vote, Stanton did not give up. She worked harder than ever. She and Susan B. Anthony put together a women's rights newspaper called *The Revolution*. It helped to get the message out.

With her children growing older, Stanton could spend more time away from home. In the 1870s, she traveled around the country making speeches.

Stanton and Anthony continued to work together as they grew older.

Stanton spoke at **conventions** and wrote articles for newspapers and magazines. She became famous for having **radical** ideas about what women should be able to do.

In 1876 Stanton and her friends wrote the Declaration of Rights for Women. It demanded "our full **equality** with man." Anthony presented it at a convention in Washington, D.C.

This is the front page of the newspaper Stanton and Anthony worked on.

Her Last Years

Stanton is seen here in 1878, the same year she spoke in front of the Senate committee. They laughed at the idea of women voting, but the fact that Stanton was allowed to speak to them was a positive step.

After 30 years of work, women still did not have the right to vote. The system of laws laid out in the U.S. **Constitution** still said that only male citizens could vote. But Elizabeth did not give up. She continued to make speeches and write articles until she died.

In 1878 Elizabeth wrote an **amendment,** or change, to the Constitution. She brought it before a U.S. Senate **committee,** but they did not vote it into law. After that, **legislators** continued to introduce the amendment in Congress until women got the right to vote.

Stanton became a powerful national leader. In 1888 she organized the International Council of Women, which was the largest women's **convention** of its time. In 1890, she became president of the National American Woman Association.

Elizabeth Cady Stanton died on October 26, 1902. It was two weeks before her 87th birthday.

Stanton worked with Anthony up until her death.

Remembering Stanton

The Nineteenth **Amendment** of 1920 gave women the right to vote. Elizabeth Cady Stanton did not live to see that law passed. She did not ever vote in her lifetime. But she did help pass many laws that gave women more rights.

Stanton helped women start on the long road to **equality.** She helped change laws so that married women had the right to property and to **custody** of their children. She also wrote several books.

Stump speaking—

In the days of "Old Dobbin" and Derby hats Mrs. Harriet Stanton Blatch exhorted the Wall Street crowds.

Elizabeth's daughter Harriot Stanton Blatch became a **suffragist.** Here she is speaking in front of a crowd in New York around 1915.

Stanton was a strong woman and a powerful force for change. She was a **feminist** who believed that women and men should be treated equally under the law.

She was an important leader for all Americans. She believed that all people are born equal and should have the same rights. Stanton never stopped working toward her goals.

This is a statue of three important women leaders. Elizabeth Cady Stanton is on the left, Susan B. Anthony is in the middle, and Lucretia Mott is on the right.

Glossary

abolitionist person who wants to get rid of something, such as slavery

amendment change or addition to a law or rule

bloomers short skirt over loose pants, worn by women instead of a full skirt

co-ed for both boys and girls

committee small group gathered for a specific purpose

constitution laws of the land

convention large group meeting

custody legal right to take care of your children

domestic dealing with the home and the family

emancipation freedom

equality having the same rights

feminist person who believes that women should have the same rights as men

legislator person who writes and votes for laws

legislature group that makes laws

pledge formal promise or agreement

radical extreme, unusual

seminary private school

sentiment thought or attitude

suffrage right to vote

More Books to Read

Davis, Lucile. *Elizabeth Cady Stanton*. Mankato, Minn.: Bridgestone, 1998.

Mattern, Joanne. *Elizabeth Cady Stanton and Susan B. Anthony*. New York: Rosen, 2003.

McDonough, Yona Zeldis. *Sisters in Strength*. New York: Henry Holt, 2000.

Parker, Barbara Keevil. *Susan B. Anthony*. Brooklyn, N.Y.: Millbrook Press, 1998.

Places to Visit

Women's Rights National Historical Park

136 Fall Street

Seneca Falls, New York 13148

Visitor Information: (315) 568-2991

Seneca Falls Historical Society

55 Cayuga Street

Seneca Falls, New York 13148

Visitor Information: (315) 568-8412

Index

Date Due

MAR 2 4 2010			
MAR 3 1 2012			